So Many Ways to
Defend Themselves

A new way to explore the animal kingdom

Editorial Director
Caroline Fortin

Research and Editing
Martine Podesto

Documentation
Anne-Marie Labrecque

Cover Design
Épicentre

Page Setup
Lucie Mc Brearty

Illustrations
François Escalmel
Jocelyn Gardner

Translator
Gordon Martin

Copy Editing
Veronica Schami

QUÉBEC AMÉRIQUE

Run for your life!

Of all the strategies animals use to defend themselves, running away is undoubtedly the most popular. When confronted by something – or someone – larger or stronger, defenseless animals rely on the power of their legs, wings or fins. They escape in many different ways: squirrels and primates climb trees, small rodents burrow into underground tunnels, birds and bats take flight, frogs and grasshoppers make leaps worthy of the greatest Olympic champions, while octopuses and squid conceal their movements by releasing a dense cloud of ink.

The high-jump champion

The springbok, a species of antelope, is a running and long-jump champion. It can leap 15 meters in a single bound! When in danger, it jumps straight up in the air, leading the entire herd in a crazy rhythm. This antelope, which can travel very long distances without getting tired, leaves most of its exhausted predators far behind. It can attain speeds of over 80 kilometers per hour.

2

springbok antelope
Antidorcas marsupialis

Are you curious?

Kangaroos can make leaps 13 meters long, and pumas come a close second with leaps of 12 meters. Grasshoppers can jump up to 6 meters, which amounts to 200 times their own length!

Walking on water

Animals will do anything they can to escape their predators, but who would have thought an 80-centimeter-long reptile could get away by running on top of the water for several meters? The basilisk, a Central American iguana, uses the long webbed digits on its hind legs to accomplish this feat. This reptile, which is a member of the iguana family, can run at a speed of 12 kilometers an hour.

basilisk
Basiliscus vittatus

The zigzag escape

beautiful fusilier
Caesio teres

When a school of fish escapes by zigzagging, the only thing their predators see is a swarming mass moving at lightning speed. This makes it very difficult to capture an individual fish. Beautiful fusilier are fish that live in the Great Barrier Reef in Australia. When they gather into a school, they create a dizzying array of magnificent blue and golden colors that completely confuses their predators.

The frog with a parachute

Certain Indonesian frogs have webbed feet and a layer of skin that extends from the last digit to the elbow joint on each of its front limbs. This set of membranes works just like a small parachute. One of these frogs is reported to have jumped from a height of 7.3 meters. What an extraordinary way to escape a predator!

3

flying frog
Rhacophorus nigropalmatus

These ones are pretty tricky

Most animals like their food to be very fresh. Predators are very rarely interested in a dead animal, especially if they have not killed it themselves. Well aware of this, many of the small creatures larger animals prey on have developed tactics that are both surprising and amusing. They pretend to be sick, or even dead. One species of American goat faints when it senses danger, the small chameleons of Madagascar feign death in the presence of an enemy, while certain African cicadas throw themselves from the foliage they inhabit: once on the ground, they remain as still as dead insects and cannot be found.

The trickery of the opossum

The Virginia opossum is a remarkable actor. As soon as an enemy approaches, it starts growling and hissing. If this tactic fails to discourage the predator, the opossum suddenly collapses and remains perfectly still, letting its body go completely limp and keeping its eyes slightly open. It's pretending to be dead! With this great trick at its disposal, it's no wonder that this prehistoric animal has survived until the present day!

4

Virginia opossum
Didelphis virginiana

Are you curious?

The Virginia opossum is closely related to kangaroos and koala bears. Its children develop in a small pouch on the stomach of the female. It is the only marsupial native to North America.

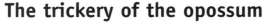

A remarkable mimic

When disturbed, the western hog-nosed
snake of America flattens its body and head
and spreads its cervical ribs, just like a
dangerous cobra. If this doesn't fool the predator,
the snake swells up with air, blows noisily and throws itself at
the aggressor, as if it's about to bite. If this routine fails to
impress the enemy, the snake feigns death: it writhes around,
turns itself belly-up, throws its head back and opens its mouth.
It's quite a show! Who would want to eat a dead snake?

western hog-nosed snake
Heterodon nasicus

A bird with an act

Certain birds, such as the killdeer, fool their
predators by pretending to be injured. The
strategy is simple: when the female senses that
an enemy is approaching the nest, she gets out
and limps away, allowing one wing to hang down as if it's broken. The
enemy follows, quite pleased to have found an easy target. But as
soon as the predator is ready to take its first bite, its meal
suddenly flies away. Sometimes an overconfident
taker is easily taken in! The dangerous intruder is
now far from the nest, and the baby birds are
out of harm's way.

killdeer
Charadrius vociferus

5

These ones make themselves look scary

Animals that can't run away sometimes stake everything on giving their attackers a good fright. Some of them display brightly colored organs that surprise and confuse their enemies. Others open their mouths up very wide, pound the ground with their tails, or whistle or jump while rolling their eyes wildly. Still others make terrifying sounds or dazzle their adversaries with blinding flashes of light. This tactic often works like a charm: the predator is surprised, confused or even disgusted by the behavior of its future meal. When confronted by such bizarre creatures, predators often choose to leave.

A surprising fan

Certain animals escape their enemy's grasp by changing the shape of their bodies or by suddenly displaying previously hidden structures. The frilled lizard has a large mantle of skin around its head. This membrane, which is usually folded against its body, spreads out like a fan at the first hint of danger. The animal just has to open its mouth. This magnificent, colorful collar makes the animal look larger and more dangerous than it actually is.

frilled lizard
Chlamydosaurus kingii

6

Are you curious?

The frilled lizard is a reptile that lives in Australia and Papua New Guinea. It eats insects, spiders and small mammals. When fleeing its predators, it can run upright on its two hind legs.

yellow-bellied toad
Bombina variegata

A little secret-keeper

Who would have guessed this drab-looking toad was hiding a brilliantly colored little belly? When disturbed, the yellow-bellied toad changes its profile in a curious way: it hollows out its back, puts its hands over its eyes and lifts its feet onto its back. If the predator persists, the toad turns over and displays its bright-yellow belly. This scares the predator because it no longer recognizes its prey.

The transformation of a caterpillar

This green caterpillar usually goes undetected among the willow leaves on which it feeds. But watch out! When it feels threatened, this charming little insect becomes a real monster. It lifts the back of its body and puffs up its red-trimmed face, revealing two false black eyes. At the tip of its body, a red fork mimics a snake's tongue and releases a strong odor.

puss moth caterpillar
Cerura vinula

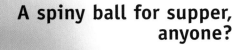

A spiny ball for supper, anyone?

Bridled burrfish live very near coral reefs in tropical seas. When disturbed, these fish can suddenly fill their stomachs with water to make themselves as round as balls, causing spines that normally lie flat against their bodies to stick up. This transformation makes them less than appetizing. Pity the poor predator who dares to make a meal of this spiny ball!

bridled burrfish
Chilomycterus antennatus

These ones can defend themselves against anything

Armed with forbidding teeth, sharp claws or pointed horns, some animals are masters of combat. Hoofed animals can rip an enemy open with a single kick. The sturdy beaks of birds, the antlers and horns of deer, gazelles and oxen, as well as the defenses of elephants and walruses, easily discourage adversaries.

An impenetrable wall

The muskox, a close relative of goats and sheep, lives in the Arctic regions of North America and Greenland. This courageous animal retreats from no enemy. Between its eyes is a plate as hard as steel that links its two horns, which can grow to be 60 centimeters long. When a wolf or bear approaches, the herd of oxen becomes a veritable fortress. The animals form a circle: the healthy adults stand on the periphery with their heads and horns pointing outward, protecting the young animals in the center of the circle.

muskox
Ovibos moschatus

8

Are you curious?

The muskox has longer hair than any other wild animal currently in existence. While the maximum length of the hair on its back is about 16 centimeters, the hair on its chest and neck can grow to be 90 centimeters long! A shaven muskox can die of pneumonia.

A formidable sword

The backs of certain kinds of rays are equipped with one or more large spines. These sword-like structures are very pointed and have serrated edges. To defend themselves, rays plunge their spines into the bodies of their attackers. The spines snap off and remain embedded in the flesh, creating a very painful wound. The spine of the southern stingray is present at birth. It can grow to be 35 centimeters long.

southern stingray
Dasyatis americana

A weapon beneath the skin

The sharp-ribbed newt or Spanish ribbed newt is a member of the Salamandridae family that inhabits Spain and northern Africa. When it is under attack, its poison-covered ribs lengthen and poke through special little pores in the skin, piercing the walls of its poor hungry predator's mouth. Any animal that dares to bite into one of these salamanders will never forget the unfortunate experience.

sharp-ribbed newt
Pleurodeles waltlii

9

Floating knives

The bodies of some fish are adorned with small blade-like structures that can seriously injure their enemies. The belly of the razorfish is as sharp as a surgeon's scalpel. When a predator approaches, these formidable little floating knives form a school and assume a vertical position, pointing their heads downward to reveal their razor-sharp bellies.

razorfishes
Centriscus scutatus

Some animals even have
chemical weapons

Several animal species are veritable little chemical factories: they have special organs that manufacture a potent mixture of toxic substances capable of scaring off predators. This phenomenon is most common among insects, fish, amphibians and reptiles, but it is also found in invertebrates like jellyfish and octopuses – as well as in certain mammals and even in one species of bird! Venomous animals have special poison-producing glands. Whether they bite, sting or spit, all these animals use a specially designed instrument to inject their toxic brew. Some of them, including the scorpion and the bee, are equipped with stings, while others have special venomous fangs or, in the case of animals like the jellyfish, long poison-injecting filaments.

black-necked spitting cobra
Naja nigricollis

A spitter of poison

Snakes are among the most dangerous venomous animals in the world. Several species of cobra, known as "spitting cobras", spit only to defend themselves. They have venomous fangs with little holes through which they squirt their poison onto lizards, small mammals and even human beings. The spitting cobra always aims its poison at shiny objects; that's why it often ends up in the eyes of the snake's enemies. They can shoot their poison up to 3 meters!

The sting of the scorpion

Closely related to spiders, scorpions inhabit hot, dry regions. They have a poison-producing "gourd" on their tails. When a scorpion is disturbed, it raises its abdomen above its head, lifts up its tail, sticks its curved sting into its enemy and injects its dangerous venom. Although very painful for humans, the sting of the scorpion is rarely fatal.

scorpion
Scorpionidae family

A shrewd fish

The stonefish of Australia is a crafty little character that hides away on the rocky floors of calm seas. Immobile and lazy, it looks like just another rock on the seabed. But watch where you put your feet! The stonefish has venomous glands on each of the spines of its dorsal fin. Its sting is horribly painful and can even lead to death. It is the most poisonous fish in the sea.

stonefish
Synanceja verrucosa

No swimming

Dangerous cubomedusa jellyfish, also known as "sea wasps", are the most dangerous animals on earth. They are found in Asian seas and off the coasts of Australia. Their tentacles are 3 meters long and inoculate victims with venom that can kill humans in less than 15 minutes. The venom from a single cubomedusa can kill as many as 60 people.

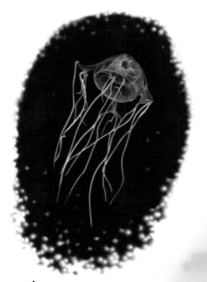

cubomedusa
Chiropsalmus quadrigatus

Are you curious?

There are over 2,700 species of snakes, 300 of which are poisonous. The venomous species include cobras, coral snakes, vipers, rattlesnakes, sea snakes and certain grass snakes. The most dangerous of all is the black-headed sea snake.

... And so are these ...

Camouflage is the best way for animals that want to survive to go unnoticed. However, animals that taste bad, or whose flesh is irritating or even lethal, are usually quite visible. Their bright markings serve as a warning. They send a very clear message: "Watch out! I'm dangerous!" A bird that has bitten into a wasp will never forget the little insect with the black and yellow bands. Nor will a predator that has encountered a skunk succeed in erasing the memory of the animal's black and white stripes – or the horrible stench of its stinky spray.

An unforgettable odor

There are nine species of skunk on the American continent. These charming little animals are armed with a very unique weapon. When a skunk feels threatened, it stamps its feet on the ground, raises its tail and points its rear end at its enemy. And if this warning is insufficient, the skunk shoots a burning stream of liquid into the eyes of its predator. This substance, which is stored in two pouches on either side of the animal's rectum, irritates the nose and the mouth – and leaves a lasting impression.

12

Are you curious?

The malodorous substance produced by the skunk is called "mercaptobutyl". It can be projected from 3 to 10 meters with great precision.

striped skunk
Mephitis mephitis

Frogs with poison darts

Small dendrobates are not only the most colorful frogs in the world, they are also the most poisonous. The venom produced by their skin glands is so powerful that the Indians of the Amazon smeared it on the points of the lances and arrows they used for protection and for hunting small game. The venom from just one of these frogs is said to be enough to coat the heads of 50 arrows!

arrow-poison frog
Phyllobates vittatus

marbled cone
Conus marmoreus

Beware of the dangerous shell

Don't touch that pretty shell! Although marbled cone look completely harmless, their beauty conceals a very real danger. These mollusks have a harpoon-shaped sting that penetrates the flesh of their victims. The powerful venom numbs or paralyzes, and sometimes kills, the victim. Unfortunately, there is no known antidote for this poison.

Strange explosions

Bombardier beetles are little living "bombs" that are very aptly named. The 12-millimeter-long bodies of these coleopterous insects contain a variety of chemical substances, each of which is stored in a separate, carefully sealed chamber. When attacked by an amphibian or a bird, the bombardier opens these chambers, the chemicals mix together and… BANG! An explosion of foul-smelling and irritating jets of vapor is released from a small tube at the tip of the animal's abdomen.

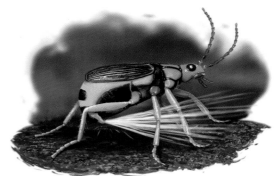

bombardier
Brachinus crepitans

Some animals have mastered
the art of camouflage

In nature, defenseless animals like to go unnoticed. The more visible they are, the more likely they are to be discovered and devoured. To avoid being spotted, the animal can of course remain perfectly still. But there is often much more to it than that! Many animals have exactly the same coloring as the environment they inhabit. Take a closer look at a tree trunk, moss, dead leaves, sand, mud, gravel or foliage: these things often conceal an insect, a frog, a fish or even a bird!

Drifting seaweed

In the case of certain animals, the patterns formed by their markings and the shape of their bodies disguise their silhouettes so well that they become practically invisible to their predators. The sea dragon is a sea horse that lives just off the coast of Australia. Its body, which looks exactly like a clump of seaweed, cannot be distinguished from the surrounding vegetation.

leafy sea dragon
Phyllopteryx eques

Are you curious?

In North America, Asia and Europe, sea horses are caught, dried and painted, then sold as trinkets. As a result of this unfortunate custom, sea-horse populations have been drastically reduced in many parts of the world.

A frog in dead leaves

Frogs are champion camouflage artists. Their markings look just like the mud, moss, bark and grass on which they live. The horned frog of Malaysia is a very small amphibian that is barely 2.5 centimeters long. When it remains still among dead leaves, this beautiful ocher- and chocolate-colored frog is exceptionally difficult to spot.

horned frog
Ceratophrys appendicula

A see-through body

Several species of small fish are almost perfectly invisible: the only thing predators see when they look at their transparent bodies is the surrounding environment. The glass catfish, found in the waters of Indo-China and Indonesia, is practically imperceptible. If you look at it very closely, you can see the bones, the spine and a few organs. But if it remains immobile in its environment, this little fish cannot be detected.

15

glass catfish
Kryptopterus bicirrhis

Like a reed in the wind

The American bittern lives in the vegetation along the banks of rivers. When it senses danger, the bird stands stock-still, turning its neck and head in the same direction as the stems of the surrounding reeds. When the wind is strong, the bird's long, striped neck sways in time with the reeds. The bittern is then perfectly camouflaged: it can observe its predator without fear of being detected.

American bittern
Botaurus lentiginosus

Some animals change their costumes

To camouflage themselves in a way that is perfectly suited to their environment, some animals, such as birds and mammals, change color from one season to the next. As its name suggests, the American varying hare varies in color depending on the season. In winter, its brown fur becomes spotlessly white, making it very easy for the hare to hide in the snow. Desert animals are the color of the sand, mountain animals are more brightly colored, while those that live in rocky areas are gray. Some reptiles, amphibians and fish are veritable magicians and change color like we change clothes, depending on their mood or the colors in their environment.

Spectacular changes of color

Octopuses and cuttlefish can change the color of their skin in just two-thirds of a second, using the pigments contained in small skin cells known as chromatophores. Depending on the surroundings, the pigments inside the chromatophores become more dispersed or more concentrated, creating a camouflage perfectly adapted to the changing environment of these animals.

16

common cuttlefish
Sepia officinalis

Are you curious?

The enemies of the cuttlefish include sharks, rays, dolphins, seals and sea birds, as well as humans who appreciate the taste of its flesh. In most cases, the cuttlefish can escape by releasing a cloud of ink. This ink can be processed to make sepia, one of the colors commonly found on painters' palettes.

Invisible on the ocean floor

Flatfish such as flounder, turbot, sole, plaice and brill can also change the color of their skin. Using cells controlled by their nervous systems, these fish can make themselves look like the sand, the gravel and even the pieces of shell found on the ocean floors on which they live.

wide-eye flounder
Bothus podas

graceful chameleon
Chamaeleo gracilis

As changeable as a chameleon

The chameleon changes color depending on its environment, the temperature, the amount of light and even its mood. This allows it to elude its predators. In only two minutes, this tree-dwelling reptile can change its spots and the color of its skin. Each of the 70 species of chameleons found in Africa, Europe and Asia has its own unique range of colors.

A crab in disguise

The hermit sea crab is a soft-bodied crustacean found on the sandy ocean floors of the eastern Atlantic, as well as throughout the Mediterranean. To protect itself, it borrows the empty shell of a mollusk and, once inside, moves around in complete security. But since its body continues to grow, the hermit crab eventually has to leave its original dwelling behind and look for a more spacious home.

hermit sea crab
Pagurus calidus

These ones are
completely invisible

To perfect the way they camouflage themselves, many animals take on the shape and appearance of an object in their immediate environment. Several grasshoppers, butterflies, chameleons, frogs, toads and fish imitate leaves with disconcerting precision. Certain caterpillars make themselves look like branches. Thorns, seeds, lichen, flowers and even bird droppings are among the many disguises animals have adopted to hide from their predators.

Butterflies that look like dead leaves

The topsides of leaf butterflies are very colorful. But when these insects are at rest, with their wings folded on their backs, they look just like dead leaves. Their unspread wings – which have leaf-like jagged edges and veins, as well as marks that look like patches of mold – hold no attraction for predators hunting for live animals.

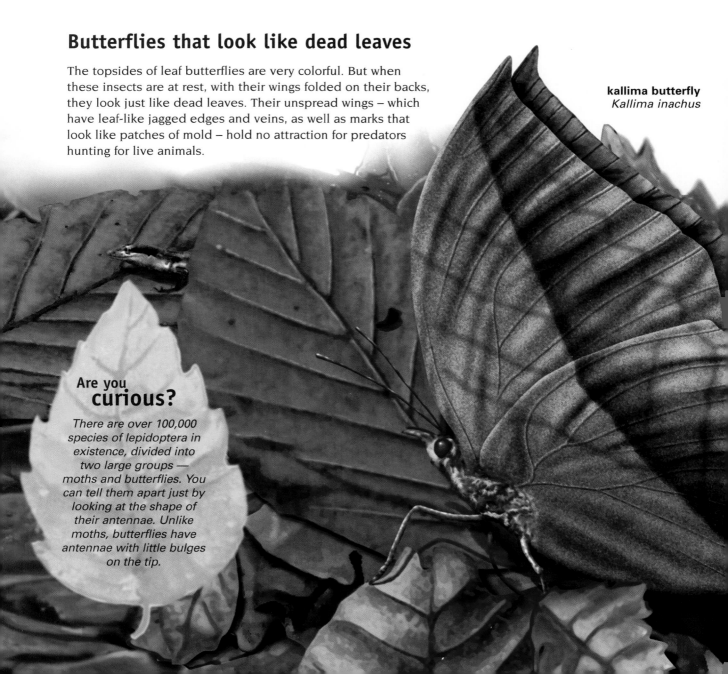

kallima butterfly
Kallima inachus

Are you curious?

There are over 100,000 species of lepidoptera in existence, divided into two large groups — moths and butterflies. You can tell them apart just by looking at the shape of their antennae. Unlike moths, butterflies have antennae with little bulges on the tip.

A dead branch or a bird?

During the day, when resting on its perch in a tree, the tawny frogmouth is well hidden from birds of prey and foxes. When it senses danger is approaching, the bird extends its neck and head, points its beak in the air and closes its eyes until they are no more than two thin slits. More often than not, this position and the color of its feathers fool its predators into mistaking it for a dead branch.

tawny frogmouth
Podargus strigoides

Giant mimics

The largest insects in the world, phasmids or stick insects, are extraordinary mimics. These giants, which can measure up to 40 centimeters long, are found mainly in the tropical regions of Asia. Not only is their coloring identical to that of the environment in which they live, their bodies mimic the shapes of leaves, branches or lichen with astonishing perfection.

giant spiny stick insect
Extatosoma tiaratum

19

Acrobatic caterpillars

The long, thin bodies of lappet-moth caterpillars look exactly like branches. Their twig-colored skin is covered with little bud-like bulges. To avoid being noticed, these acrobats rely on a remarkable camouflage technique. They firmly grip the limb of a tree with their hind legs, then let their bodies hang down like small branches.

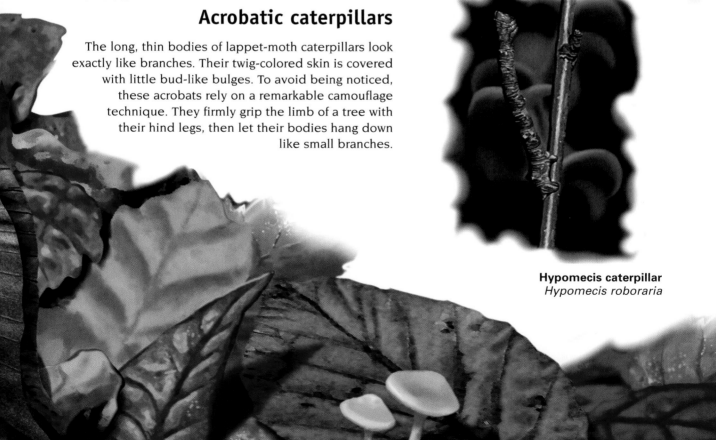

Hypomecis caterpillar
Hypomecis roboraria

Some even pass themselves
off as other animals

Many harmless animals adopt the colors of certain dangerous, poisonous or foul-tasting species. This disguise protects these otherwise defenseless animals from predators, who think they're dealing with a much more dangerous species. This tactic, which is known as "mimicry", is particularly common among insects, but is also used by certain mammals and snakes.

Which one is the impostor?

The American coral snake has an almost perfect double. But be careful! It's important to learn to tell them apart. The coral snake is poisonous – it can kill many animals and is very dangerous for humans – whereas the king snake is completely harmless. However, since both species are adorned with yellow, black and red bands, they inspire the same terror in all their predators.

coral snake
Micrurus nigrocinctus

hoverfly
Chrysotoxum cautum

common wasp
Vespula vulgaris

Would-be wasps and bogus bees

The insects belonging to the Syrphidae family are closely related to ordinary flies. But the shape and color of these harmless insects are very much like those of bees and wasps. These little tricksters can thus gather nectar without fear of being disturbed.

Lookalikes

When attacked by another animal, the African zorilla turns its back and, just like its cousin the skunk, soaks the unfortunate aggressor with a foul-smelling liquid stored in its anal pockets. The maned rat, which inhabits the same regions as the zorilla, also has a black-and-white coat. And when disturbed, it too displays the hairs on its back. Its zorilla-like markings save it a great deal of trouble.

zorilla
Ictonyx striatus

maned rat
Lophiomys imhausi

21

sinaloan milksnake
Lampropeltis triangulum sinaloae

Are you curious?

So you think it's hard to tell the difference between the real one and the fake? Look carefully: on the dreaded poisonous coral snake, yellow bands are always next to red ones, but on the impostor, these bands are always separated by a black band.

These ones have
impenetrable armor

Certain animals wear coats of protective armor. Elephants, hippopotami and rhinoceroses are covered by a sturdy layer of skin, while crustaceans, mollusks, turtles, anteaters and armadillos hide behind veritable shields. Several small mammals such as echidnas, tenrecs and hedgehogs are equipped with superb spine-covered coats. Rather than fleeing their enemies, these mammals brandish their spines like a multitude of small sharp weapons.

An unrecognizable animal

The body of the armadillo is ringed by bands of bony plates separated by rows of hair. Using this supple shield, the three-banded armadillo can roll itself into a ball with lightning speed, making itself unrecognizable and, above all, inedible. When in danger, some armadillos rapidly dig a hole in the ground and take refuge there, holding their breath for up to six long minutes!

southern three-banded armadillo
Tolypeutes matacus

A giant pine cone

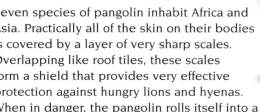

Seven species of pangolin inhabit Africa and Asia. Practically all of the skin on their bodies is covered by a layer of very sharp scales. Overlapping like roof tiles, these scales form a shield that provides very effective protection against hungry lions and hyenas. When in danger, the pangolin rolls itself into a ball or pounds the ground with its tail and sprays the enemy with a foul-smelling stream of liquid produced by the glands near its tail.

Malayan pangolin
Manis javanica

The devil of the desert

A member of the iguana family, this lizard is not a very attractive food option for the predators of Australian deserts and steppes. Its body is covered with large spiny scales and a thorn protrudes from a large bulge on the nape of its neck. When confronted by an enemy, this creature bows its head and points the horn-like thorn on its hump at the adversary. This must be why it was given the name "thorny devil".

thorny devil
Moloch horridus

Dangerous needles

The North American porcupine is a ball of 30,000 spines that stand on end at the first sign of danger. Once they enter the skin of the enemy, these needles, which can be up to 5 centimeters long, penetrate deeper and deeper into the flesh: they can even pierce organs, sometimes killing the victim. Baby porcupines are born with flat, flaccid spines that harden quickly as they dry out.

Are you curious?

Armadillos, pangolins, anteaters and sloths belong to a group known as the "edentate" or "toothless" mammals. However, this classification is inappropriate because pangolins and anteaters are the only members of the group that don't have any teeth.

North American porcupine
Erethizon dorsatum

These ones give up their arms

Some animals leave their predators with nothing but a wriggling piece of their body. This phenomenon, which is known as "autotamy", is present among several invertebrates such as earthworms, starfish, crabs and mollusks, which can cast off then regenerate one or more parts of their bodies. Autotamy is also common among reptiles: snakes and even crocodiles can shed and replace the tips of their tails.

Limbs that grow back

When in danger, many crabs abandon a claw, or one or more legs, and run for cover. The next time it molts, the crab emerges from this transformation with brand-new claws and legs. Some crabs implant their claws in the flesh of their predators, leaving them to deal with the consequences.

edible crab
Cancer pagurus

Are you curious?

Lizards use their tails for running, climbing, swimming and maintaining their balance. Those without tails don't live as long as those with tails.

A detachable tail

Most species of lizard can detach a portion of their tail when in danger. While this piece continues to wriggle around in the mouth of the surprised enemy, the lizard runs away at top speed. Shortly after this misadventure, the lost tail is replaced by a new, albeit shorter, one.

Pacific western skink
Leiolopisma laterimaculata

Feathers...

Severe fright doesn't only make hairs stand on end, it also makes feathers fall out! A strange phenomenon, fear-related molting, has been observed in several bird species. When they are very scared, birds such as cardinals can shed some of their feathers. These abandoned feathers fly around, creating a diversion that disconcerts the predator and allows the bird to escape.

northern cardinal
Cardinalis cardinalis

Dismembered stars...

Many simple animals such as worms and starfish can separate themselves from parts of their bodies and some of them can regenerate the missing pieces. Starfish can cast off one or more arms when under attack. They then swim away, leaving their thwarted enemies with nothing but detached limbs. However, these limbs do not grow back in all species of starfish.

common sun-star
Crossaster papposus

More clues for
the most curious

ONCE BITTEN, TWICE SHY		
Method of injecting poison	**Animal**	**Toxicity for humans**
Bite	Black widow (*Latrodectus mactans*)	Rarely dangerous (deaths are usually the result of nervous shock)
	Mojave rattlesnake (*Crotalus scutulatus*)	Extremely dangerous
	Gila monster (*Heloderma suspectum*)	Rarely dangerous
	Marine bloodworm (*Glycera dibranchiata*)	Slightly irritating
	Sea snake (Hydrophiidae family)	Very dangerous (but rare and not very aggressive)
Sting	Scorpion (Scorpionidae family)	Rarely dangerous
	Duckbill platypus (*Ornithorynchus anatinus*)	Dangerous
	Cubomedusa (*Chiropsalmus quadrigatus*)	Very irritating
	Sea anemone (several species)	Very irritating
Contact or ingestion	Arrow-poison frogs (*Dendrobates* and *Phyllobates* genera)	Extremely dangerous if eaten
	Blowfish (Tetraodontidae family)	Dangerous if the liver, gonads, viscera or eggs are eaten
	Newt (*Notophthalmus* genus)	Dangerous if eaten
	Marine toad (*Bufo marinus*)	Very irritating
Spitting	Spitting cobra (*Naja nigricollis* or *Naja mozambica*)	Very irritating for the eyes

KEY

Slightly irritating: Redness, swelling, minor local pain.

Very irritating: Burning sensation, itching, serious pain, temporary blindness.

Rarely dangerous: Rarely causes death among healthy adults, can be fatal for children, seniors and people with failing health. Can cause local pain, numbness, nausea, vomiting, breathing problems, temporary paralysis.

Dangerous: Local pain, numbness, local edema.

Very dangerous: Serious local pain, excessive salivation, fever, delirium, extreme agitation, loss of consciousness, serious edema, blackening of extremities, loss of fingers and toes.

Extremely dangerous: Fatal.

TRICKING TRICKSTERS...

Animal	Means of defense	Predators	Explanations
Horned frog	Camouflage	Birds of prey and snakes	Birds of prey and snakes use their sense of smell for hunting.
Venomous caterpillars	Venom	Cuckoos	Cuckoos are not affected by the poison of venomous caterpillars and even less so by their horrible taste.
Bees and wasps	Sting and venom	Bee-eaters	These birds disarm bees and wasps by removing their stings.
Ants	Acidic taste	Anteaters and woodpeckers	This mammal and this bird are protected against the acid in ants' bodies.
Bombardier	Irritating spray	Rodents	Many rodents rub the abdomens of bombardiers against the ground, thus preventing the beetles from spraying their jet of irritating fluid.
Snakes and scorpions	Venom	Hornbills	Hornbills crush snakes and scorpions with the tips of their beaks, thus destroying their venomous organ.
Electric ray	Electric current	Moray eels	Morays can withstand electric currents.
Nine-banded armadillo	Shell	Jaguars	Jaguars are among the only large carnivores capable of "unfolding" the tight ball formed by the bodies of armadillos.
Cuttlefish	Camouflage	Sharks and rays	Sharks and rays eat cuttlefish when the mollusks are swimming in search of food.

DO YOU KNOW?

1. How can Amazonian bats that hunt at night distinguish between poisonous and edible frogs?
2. Are chameleons the only reptiles that can change color to match their surroundings?
3. Do bright markings always indicate that an animal is venomous or is mimicking a venomous species?
4. Can all animals that use autotamy as a means of defense regenerate their lost tails or arms?
5. If camouflaging coats help animals hide from predators, why do terns, oyster catchers and deer lose their camouflage when they reach adulthood?

*Answers at the end of Glossary (p. 31).

For further
information...

springbok antelope
Antidorcas marsupialis

class Mammalia
order Artiodactyla
family Bovidae

size and weight	95 to 115 cm; 25 to 46 kg
distribution	southern Africa
habitat	arid open plains
diet	grasses
reproduction	1 baby per litter
predators	lions, cheetahs, hyenas

Virginia opossum
Didelphis virginiana

class Mammalia
order Marsupialia
family Didelphidae

size and weight	25 to 45 cm, including the tail; 2 to 5.5 kg
distribution	South America, eastern United States, southeastern Canada
habitat	deciduous forests, tropical forests, prairies, mountains, urban areas
diet	grasses, fruit, nuts, reptiles, small mammals
reproduction	up to 20 babies per litter, 12- to 14-day pregnancies

frilled lizard
Chlamydosaurus kingii

class Reptilia
order Lepidosauria
family Agamidae

size	80 to 90 cm, including the tail
distribution	Australia, Papua New Guinea
habitat	savannas and wooded areas of desert regions
diet	insects, spiders, small mammals
predators	snakes, birds of prey

muskox
Ovibos moschatus

class Mammalia
order Artiodactyla
family Bovidae

size and weight	180 to 245 cm; 350 to 650 kg
distribution	from Alaska to Greenland
habitat	Arctic regions and tundra near glaciers
diet	arctic willow, silvery cinquefoil, catchflies
reproduction	1 baby per female every 1 or 2 years
predators	wolves, polar bears

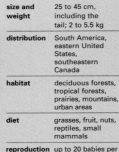

black-necked spitting cobra
Naja nigricollis

class Reptilia
order Squamatidae
family Elapidae

size	up to 2 m long
distribution	from central to southern Africa
habitat	savannas and arid wooded regions
diet	small mammals, birds, eggs, snakes, batrachians
reproduction	12 to 20 eggs at a time
predators	birds of prey, reptiles, hornbills, mongooses
life span	15 to 20 years in captivity

striped skunk
Mephitis mephitis

class Mammalia
order Carnivora
family Mustelidae

size and weight	50 to 70 cm, including the tail; 1.5 to 3 kg
distribution	southern Canada, United States, northern Mexico
habitat	forests, plains, prairies, thickets, suburban areas
diet	insects, small mammals, larvae, bird eggs and fruit
predators	birds of prey

leafy sea dragon
Phyllopteryx eques

class Osteichtheyes
order Gasterostei-formes
family Syngnathidae

size	up to 20 cm long
distribution	Australia
habitat	soft bottoms of coastal waters
diet	small fish, crustaceans, plankton
reproduction	200 eggs at a time, incubated by the male for 4 weeks

common cuttlefish
Sepia officinalis

class Cephalopoda
order Decapoda
family Sepiidae

size	10 to 65 cm
distribution	Atlantic, English Channel, North Sea and Mediterranean
habitat	coastal waters
diet	fish, crustaceans and mollusks
reproduction	over 500 eggs at a time
predators	sharks, sea bass, dolphins, rays, hakes, seals, cetaceans, diving birds

kallima butterfly
Kallima inachus

class Insecta
order Lepidoptera
family Nymphalidae

size	4 to 5 cm
distribution	Asia, especially the Indo-Australian region
habitat	wooded areas, bamboo undergrowth
diet	flower nectar, plant gap
reproduction	several hundred eggs per laying season
predators	birds, reptiles, small mammals

sinaloan milksnake
Lampropeltis triangulum sinaloae

class Reptilia
order Squamatidae
family Colubridae

size	up to 2 m long
distribution	United States, Central America, Ecuador
habitat	swamp forests, riverbanks, prairies, semiarid deserts
diet	small mammals, lizards, fish, eggs
predators	birds of prey, corvidae, small carnivores, serpents of the same and other species

southern three-banded armadillo
Tolypeutes matacus

class Mammalia
order Edentata
family Dasypodidae

size	35 to 46 cm, including the tail
distribution	Bolivia, Paraguay, Brazil, Argentina
habitat	grassy prairies
diet	small vertebrates and insects
reproduction	1 baby per litter
predators	foxes, wolves, dogs
life span	12 to 15 years

edible crab
Cancer pagurus

class Crustacae
order Decapoda
family Cancridae

size and weight	20 cm; up to 6 kg
distribution	Atlantic and Mediterranean
habitat	rocky bottoms up to depths of 90 m
diet	scallops, oysters, mussels, gastropods, barnacles
reproduction	up to 3 million eggs
predators	octopuses, lobsters, bottomfish, sharks, rays
life span	10 years

Glossary

Abdomen

Lower portion of the trunk containing the digestive organs. In invertebrates, the abdomen corresponds to the end of the body.

Amphibian

Animal, such as the frog, that can live on land or in water.

Anal pouches

Small bag-shaped cavities located near the anus.

Antidote

Remedy for a poison.

Autotamy

Casting off of a body part to escape a predator.

Bulge

Rounded swelling, outward curve.

Coleopteron

Insect in which the forewings are protected by other harder wings when at rest.

Coral reef

Ridge of limestone made up of coral skeletons.

Forelimb

Front limb.

Gland

Organ that produces a secretion, a relatively thick liquid.

Habitation

Dwelling or location that can be lived in.

Invertebrate

Any animal lacking a backbone.

Mammal

Any species in which the female has mammary glands to feed her young.

Marsupial

Any mammal in which the female has a stomach pouch containing mammary glands, where the newly born offspring can be carried and suckled.

Membrane

Thin layer of living cells.

Mollusk

A soft-bodied invertebrate living on land or in water, such as the snail, the mussel or the octopus.

Nervure

Thin raised vein or rib on the surface of the leaf of a plant.

Overlapping

Partly covering each other.

Periphery

Edge, border.

Pigment

Naturally occurring colored substance.

Predator

Animal that feeds on prey.

Prehistoric

Before the development of writing and the use of metals.

Primates

Mammals, such as apes, with a full set of teeth and hands that can grip objects.

Protrude

To stick out or jut out.

Reptile

Crawling animal with scale-covered skin, such as the snake, the iguana and the turtle.

Sting

Sharp pointed organ that insects like bees use to inject poison.

Substance

Hard or soft material, solid or liquid.

Syrphidae

Family of insects with yellow and black abdomens that includes wasps and bees.

Tentacle

Long flexible arm of certain mollusks used to touch and grab, and often equipped with suckers.

Vegetation

The plant life of a particular region.

ANSWERS TO "DO YOU KNOW?" QUIZ

1. Bats apparently avoid being poisoned because they can hear the shrill little screams golfodulcean poison dart frogs emit to stake their territory.
2. Many other lizards, including the green anole and numerous geckos, also have this ability.
3. Not necessarily. The purpose of colorful markings is often to attract sexual partners during the mating season, to lure prey or even to make it possible to identify members of the same species.
4. Lizards and skinks can grow new tails and many starfish can grow new arms, but some animals lose their limbs forever.
5. Once they become adults, they are faster and have many more ways to evade predators. They no longer have to lie low.

Index

The terms in **bold characters** refer to an illustration; those in *italics* indicate a key-word.

So many ways to defend themselves was created and produced by **QA International**, a division of Les Éditions Québec Amérique inc. 329, rue de la Commune Ouest, 3e étage, Montréal (Québec) H2Y 2E1 Canada **T** 514.499.3000 **F** 514.499.3010
©1998 Éditions Québec Amérique inc.

ISBN 2-89037-959-0

Printed and bound in Canada

10 9 8 7 6 5 4 3 2 1   99 98